Growing Up in N.D.G.

Growing Up in N.D.G.

BY RUSSELL BAIN

WITH SKETCHES BY JOHN COLLINS

Shoreline

Shoreline, 23 Ste-Anne
Ste-Anne-de-Bellevue, Quebec H9X 1L1
shoreline@sympatico.ca 514.457.5733 www.shorelinepress.ca

Graphic design: Anneclaire Le Royer

Printed in Canada

Dépôt légal: Library and Archives Canada
and Bibliothèque et archives nationales du Québec

Library and Archives Canada Cataloguing in Publication
Bain, Russell, 1917-2004
Growing up in N.D.G. / Russell Bain: sketches by John Collins.
ISBN 978-1-896754-53-6
1. Bain, Russell, 1917-2004 -- Childhood and youth. 2. Collins, John, 1917-2007-- Childhood and youth. 3. Notre-Dame-de-Grâce (Montréal, Québec)-- Pictorial works. 4. Notre-Dame-de-Grâce (Montréal, Québec)-- Biography. I. Collins, John, 1917- 2007. II. Title.

FC2947.25.B34 2007 971.4'28 C2007-905610-5

Russell Bain and John Collins were friends for over eighty years. They grew up on Old Orchard Avenue in N.D.G. They went to school together, played hockey, football and baseball together. They were Wolf Cubs and Boy Scouts in the same troop.

When Russ retired and moved to Kingston he took up writing as a hobby and started to recall early days in N.D.G. to let his children in other parts of Canada know something of the old area. This book is dedicated to him and those children and grandchildren to let them know a little of our small part in Montreal's history.

John Collins

Seven Wolf Cubs from Old Orchard Avenue:
Top row: Gordie Appleton, Ted Hook.
Next row: Barry Elliott, Johnny Marshall, Kay Shaw, Russ Bain.
First row: Jack Collins

N.D.G.
FRONT STEPS

Notre Dame de Grâce (sometimes translated as 'no damn good'), an area in the western part of Montreal, was where we grew up. It had been farm country in the previous century, famous for its Montreal melons so sweet they were shipped to fancy New York restaurants. After the First World War, developers moved in and the streets above Monkland Avenue west of Girouard became lined with four-unit duplex flats. Street after street extended westward: Old Orchard (where we lived), Marcil, Oxford, Harvard, Wilson. Our families moved in just after the flats were completed and while construction was going on all around us. It was a great time for little boys. After the workmen went home in the evening we could explore half-finished houses and pick up boards, nails and anything that was lying around. Young boys are always inquisitive so we would poke our noses into everything until called for homework and bedtime. Who needed playgrounds when we had buildings under construction to explore?

In the early 1900s and particularly after World War I, the city of Montreal moved westward into the Notre Dame de Grâce area. Apple orchards and sloping farmlands were laid out as city streets. Builders, contractors, politicians, and merchants moved in and the expression 'rugged individualist' would not be misused to describe any one of them.

Originally from St. Henri ward, a French Canadian with the unlikely name of Josh Hoolahan developed the whole west side of Oxford Avenue from Monkland to Somerled. He crossed that avenue, put up one more housing unit and then started an apartment house at the corner of Côte St. Luc Road. He mothballed that project when the effects of the October '29 market crash became apparent. Noted for his swings of temperament from absolute zero to the boiling point of water in less time than it took for a Montreal Tramways conductor to close his streetcar doors on a sub-zero morning, Hoolahan was not the first name to come to mind when thinking of community work. Yet, at the very bottom of the depression, he built a hockey rink and a toboggan slide on a vacant lot for the neighbourhood kids.

In 1928, Notre Dame de Grâce elected Winchester Henry Biggar as its alderman to the Montreal City Council. Known to his intimates as 'Windy', Biggar was a law graduate of McGill who, after practicing for a time, became interested in civic government. His questions at council meetings about the awarding of contracts, snow removal, building permits, and the construction of comfort stations in city parks made some of his fellow aldermen, and even the mayor himself, wriggle in their seats. At the time of his death in 1939, the *Montreal Gazette* wrote:

"One of his last civic political campaigns at the city hall was conducted against a peculiar form of civic contracts and blossomed out in what was known as 'the St. Helen's peanut concession fight'. At that time, the buying of equipment and supplies at City Hall came under his scrutiny and castigation."

Easily recognized by his distinctive bow tie, Biggar represented not only the taxpayers of Notre Dame de Grâce, but most of Montreal's business establishments at the city's meetings. This latter case was brought about by the fact that the big employers lived, almost to a man, in the separate city of Westmount, thereby having no direct voice in Montreal's affairs.

Surrounded by suburban stores and apartment houses, an old farmhouse stood by itself for years on Monkland Avenue at the corner of Marcil. Known as Brodie's Farm, the house was set back from the street under beautiful shade trees. A barn stood behind the house and beyond that was a small piece of fenced land where two apple trees grew. The barn had a loft that was home to a flock of pigeons. More than one boy hid there with cramps after eating green apples. In the evening, undeterred by spooky dog barks, we would raid the trees for fruit, with a great sense of daring and achievement. Today, the St. John's Estonian Evangelical Lutheran Church adjoins the old property.

LOOK NO HANDS
OOOOOPS
BIKE RIDING DAYS

The bicycle was a big part of boyhood in the '20s and '30s. There wasn't much auto traffic on our quiet residential street, so we could ride everywhere. We had lamps for after-dark riding, and, of course, bells. We attached cards to the spokes to create a satisfying clatter. Bikes gave some of us a chance to show off for girls on the sidewalk, occasionally leading to awkward results.

Some of us had first listened with earphones to crystal sets. But during the 1920s and '30s, most families had a radio. We listened to Fibber McGee and Molly, Eddie Cantor, Edgar Bergen and Charlie McCarthy, Amos and Andy, and a Canadian musical show, 'The Cookanoodle Club', sponsored by a chocolate company named Smiles and Chuckles. Girls swooned over Nelson Eddy and Rudy Vallée, we all followed the exploits of 'Little Orphan Annie', and sent away for decoder rings. We pestered our mothers to buy Beehive Golden Corn Syrup so we could use the labels to get into the six-day bicycle races at the Forum. If you walked down Old Orchard at seven o'clock on a summer evening, you could hear 'Amos and Andy' floating through open windows.

When Sherbrooke Street was lined with maple trees to commemorate the men killed in World War I; when boys turned wooden sugar boxes on end and nailed them to their sleighs to make winter scooters; and when Camillien Houde, who might have been selected by Gilbert and Sullivan, was mayor of Montreal -- those were the days when N.D.G. was young.

The maple trees that lined Sherbrooke Street had been planted after that First World War in honour of soldiers killed in the conflict. They aroused interest in small boys because each one had a bronze marker giving the name of a casualty of the war. We read these and wondered who they were and what they had done during their years of service. Most, if not all, of the trees and all of the memorial plaques are long gone from today's N.D.G.

Another N.D.G. landmark was 'Ma Hellers' located just across Sherbrooke Street from the Empress Theater. This snack bar was a little out of our range but was popular with teens from Trenholme Park, N.D.G. Park and Loyola. It later was known for Ma's list of N.D.G. boys serving in the forces in the Second World War.

In September 1939, Germany invaded Poland and Britain declared war. Canada instantly followed.

The telephone pole was the center of youthful activity on our street. We gathered there every day and stood around under its lights at night. The pole was 'home' for games of hide and seek.

Summers were long when we were young. You counted the days until the end of school term, but vacation time needed activities. One summer, we all made scooters; that was the year after everybody was on roller skates. Another summer, it was all yo-yo's, trying tricks like 'walking the dog' and 'around the world'. Every year, there were baseball and bikes to keep us busy. A year to remember was the 'Just Kids' card collecting craze. These cards came in chocolate bars and were drawn by cartoonist Jim Frise of 'Birdseye Center' fame. A complete set would win you a prize.

In order to complete our card collections we ate 'Just Kids' bars until we could hardly face another one. We hoarded them and swapped 'traders' to acquire the whole collection, and then to receive that long desired prize, which proved to be a mechanical pencil complete with a compass and penknife blade, none of which worked very well.

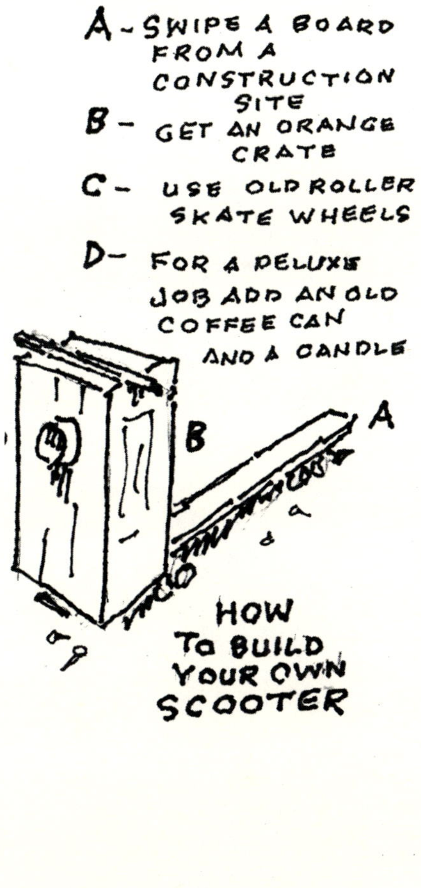
A - SWIPE A BOARD FROM A CONSTRUCTION SITE
B - GET AN ORANGE CRATE
C - USE OLD ROLLER SKATE WHEELS
D - FOR A DELUXE JOB ADD AN OLD COFFEE CAN AND A CANDLE
B
A
HOW TO BUILD YOUR OWN SCOOTER

Both boys and girls played marbles. Mostly we used the dull clay ones but treasured the shiny glass ones in glowing colours. When winter kept us indoors, we had Mecanno sets to keep us busy -- usually hunting for lost screws. Or we fooled around with balsa wood to create model planes that almost always ended up in a crash.

Some boys collected toy soldiers. Around Christmas time the big department stores had glittering displays of toy soldiers: no GI Joes in dull olive drab but Scots in bright kilts and British Grenadiers in brilliant scarlet tunics -- just the stuff to make a little boy's eyes pop and give him dreams of what he might find under the tree on Christmas morning.

When the Whelans lived where 'Li'l Loy Lan Lyke' had lived, Bill had a lot of trouble with one of his legs and I remember that he had surgery not once but several times in attempts to correct the problem. Each time he wound up in a cast and would be carried out by his family to sit on the front steps to watch the world go by. He always had games to play: Snakes and Ladders, Crokinole, Parchesi, and the like. He loved you to stop by, autograph his cast and chat, always cheerful. If memory serves me right, George Pope sort of took him under his wing.

Scabs were a big part of every boy's summer in the 1920s. All the plots of our N.D.G. flats had 'Keep Off the Grass' signs so we played in the street. We wore shorts all summer and collected a weird assortment of cuts and bruises. Curiosity made us lift the edges of scabs to see how the cuts were healing. This, of course, made them bleed all over again. This could and did go on all summer....

All of us went to the movies when we could scrape up the money. On Sunday, January 9th, 1927, the Laurier Palace Theatre had been hit by fire. In this disaster many children and adults were trampled to death. The death toll of 76 prompted the government to enact a law restricting children under the age of 16 from entering a movie house in Quebec.

We went to The Monkland and The Empress on Sherbrooke Street. The Empress, still standing, was decorated in Egyptian style with gods and pharaohs everywhere. When we went to the washroom, we felt we were entering King Tut's tomb. We always sat in the balcony, where we formed a noisy group, to the indignation of the ushers.

The OLD EMPRESS — TODAY

The MONKLAND · IN 1930

In the fall of 1931, two lads set out to earn one of Scouting's highest awards, the Pathfinder's badge. The boys were members of the 124th Boy Scout Troop, which met at St. Matthew's Anglican Church, on the border of Hampstead and N.D.G. The boys' names were Donnie Delvin and Russell Bain. In spite of the fact that they knew it was easier to earn badges at Camp Tamaracouta in the summer, where the distractions of school, homework and football didn't exist, they decided to undertake a project to map and show key locations for 'A Portion of Côte St. Luc Road'. The 'portion' they had in mind led west through pretty much open country.

Accordingly, they met on a Saturday morning in October at about ten o'clock opposite a restored farmhouse where Dufferin Road met Côte St. Luc. Their mothers had made them lunches. They had 10 cents each for a soft drink and a car ticket apiece for the return journey. Between them, they had a compass, a pedometer and a notebook.

Knowing enough to keep magnetic variation into account, they took a bearing to the middle of the road in the distance. They walked along the boundary of the Town of Hampstead on their right. Then the Sun Life tennis courts on their left. Just beyond the courts was the trunk of an old fallen oak tree. The tree had lost its bark and been dried by the wind and sun for years. It was a favorite rendezvous for a group of boys from Old Orchard Avenue near Monkland. They liked to visit the site on their bicycles and carve their initials on the trunk. The two boys noted the correct compass bearing and the pedometer reading, and all these locations were recorded.

Further out and on a fresh bearing, the boys' walk took them to an old two-story stone building. The ground level of the place was given over to a primitive version of today's convenience store or depanneur. Upstairs was an equally shabby dwelling. The whole spooky thing looked as it belonged in a Boris Karloff film. The lads tactfully called it 'Old Stone Store'.

On another bearing the Scouts came to a bridge crossing a stream running through the fields to where Westminster Avenue came up from Montreal West. A bit further west the road came to a dead end at the CPR marshalling yards in Sortin. In the Sortin Yards the railway had built an employees' recreation centre along the track. There was a nine-hole golf course, tennis courts and a roomy clubhouse. It was called Wentworth. All details jotted in their notebook, the boys found that the clubhouse would sell them soft drinks and allow them to eat their lunches on the big verandah. Here they learned to watch for cinders from the shunting locomotives.

The final stage of the mapping was to retrace their steps to the Westrminster intersection. Then one more compass reading down the avenue. A walk using the pedometer to the hog's back bridge that crossed the railway tracks. Distance recorded. Bridge noted. Notebook put away.

Over the bridge was the terminus for the #73 streetcar. Fishing out their tickets, the Scouts boarded the tram. They took transfers, changed at Girouard and so to home.

The following week they spent an evening at the Bains' dining-room table with a large sheet of white paper, a bottle of India ink, a pen, a protractor, and a ruler. From this map appeared what was identified as 'A Portion of Côte St. Luc Road'. A legend indicating the various sites appeared in the lower left-hand corner. The boys' names appeared in the lower right hand corner. The finished map was submitted at the next regular troop meeting.

In March at a 'Father and Son' banquet, where a delicious meal of corned beef hash was served up by the mothers, the two boys were called forward to proudly accept their Pathfinders badges from a beaming Scoutmaster.

BENDS AND HITCHES

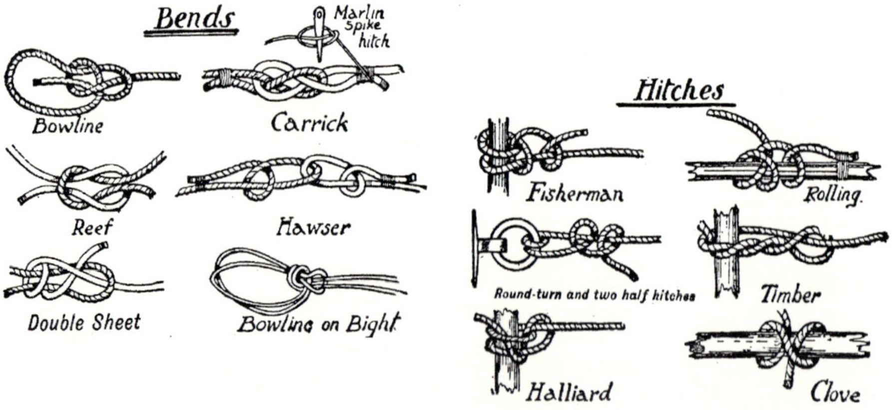

A Scout troop was divided into patrols given the names of animals. There were Wolf, Buffalo, Moose -- ours was the Fox patrol. A big Scout activity was knot tying. How many Scouts can tell the difference between a bowline and a clove hitch? We are lucky if we can tell a reef knot from a granny knot....

Part of a Scout's summer training was two weeks or more at Camp Tamaracouta, near Morin Heights in the Laurentians. We never quite caught on to Scout discipline. We never became patrol leaders, were always last in line and also usually out of step. In camp we slept in tents and on straw-filled ticks. In the main building there were offices, a mess hall and 'tuck shop' where we could buy candy bars. It was where one young scout saw his first 'art', a print of a Frederic Remington painting of U.S. calvary charging, all dust, wild-eyed horses and swinging sabers. There was this kid, sent to camp to become a woodsman, felling trees, lighting fires, tying knots and paddling canes, standing with mouth agape, thinking , "Wow, imagine being able to paint like that!"

A member of the 124th Boy Scout troop that met weekly at St. Matthew's Anglican Church was Lawrence 'Fat' Goodings. 'Fat' Goodings was good natured. He was chubby. He had street smarts. He was generally acknowledged by the other scouts to know all about women.

In 1932 the scoutmaster was F. Roberts Walker.

F. Roberts Walker was president of the James Walker hardware company, an old family business. 'Boss' Walker was a handsome man who could become very emotional at occasions like a 'Father and Son' dinner. He lived well, although word was that the hardware company was not what it had once been.

In addition to the Boy Scout troop and its affiliate Wolf Cub pack, F. Roberts Walker decided that a Rover Crew was needed to maintain the interest of some of the older boys who were getting beyond the scouting experience. Some of the new Rovers had good years of scouting under their belts, others had always been fringe members of the troop. One never would wear the full Boy Scout uniform. Another seemed to qualify because he had been the first to lose his virginity. The Rovers were not a group to be thought of with unqualified regard.

Morals plummeted. A substitute scoutmaster who stuttered was actually booed by some of the boys. F. Roberts Walker was said to have wept over the incident. The offenders were made to repeat the Scout's Promise at a special meeting, but things were never the same and the boys gradually drifted away.

The wayward Scouts had been shamed. For his part, F. Roberts Walker was promoted to District Scout Commissioner.

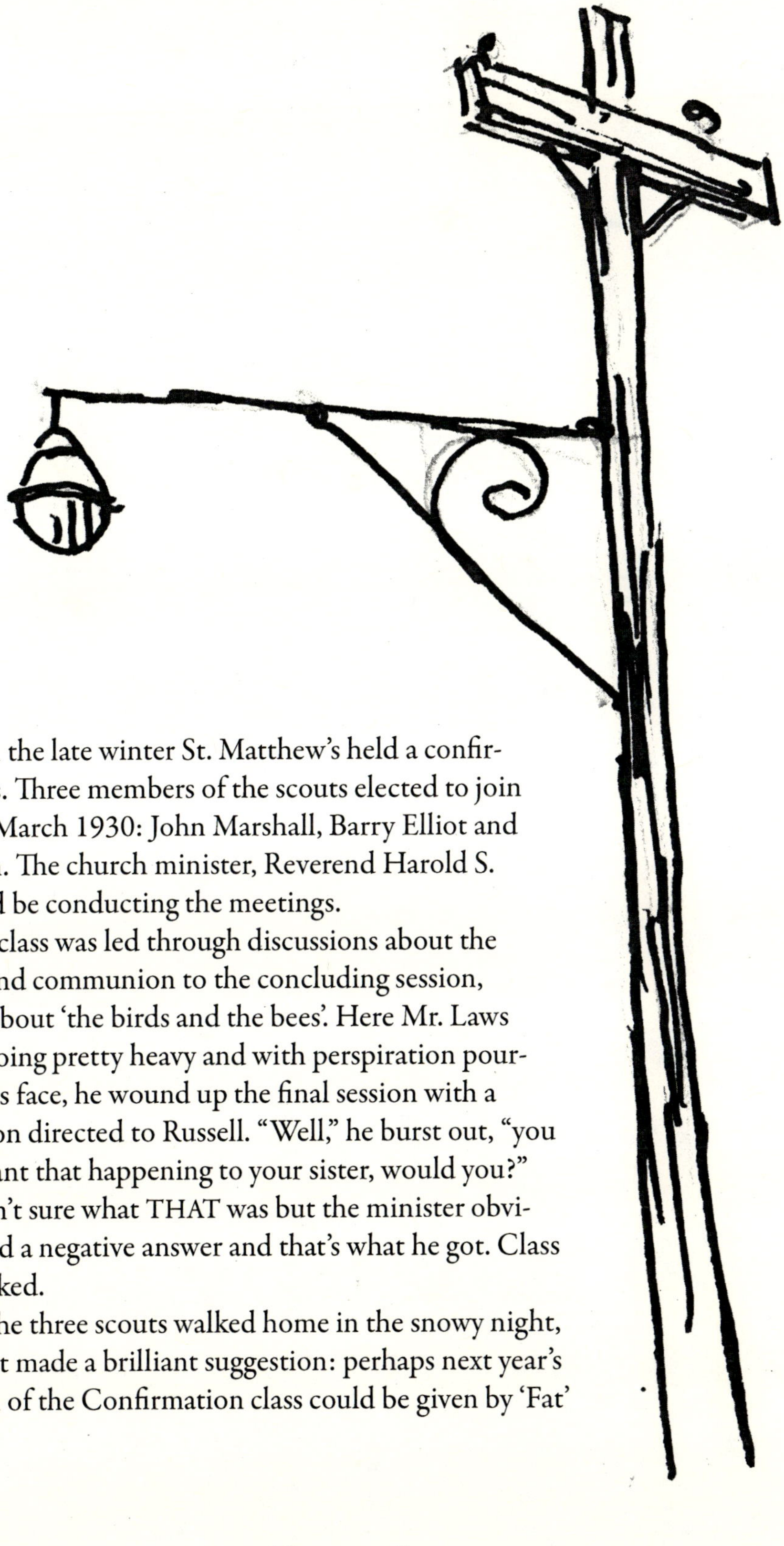

Each year in the late winter St. Matthew's held a confirmation class. Three members of the scouts elected to join the class in March 1930: John Marshall, Barry Elliot and Russell Bain. The church minister, Reverend Harold S. Laws, would be conducting the meetings.

The class was led through discussions about the catechism and communion to the concluding session, which was about 'the birds and the bees'. Here Mr. Laws found the going pretty heavy and with perspiration pouring down his face, he wound up the final session with a loud question directed to Russell. "Well," he burst out, "you wouldn't want that happening to your sister, would you?" Russell wasn't sure what THAT was but the minister obviously wanted a negative answer and that's what he got. Class interest peaked.

As the three scouts walked home in the snowy night, Barry Elliott made a brilliant suggestion: perhaps next year's final session of the Confirmation class could be given by 'Fat' Gooding....

Long before we had push button or even dial phones we had to call central for a line and switchboard operators would connect us. Bell had divided the city into interchanges with different names. We used telephones coloured as Henry Ford said of his Model T, "You can have it in any colour as long as it's black.'

We rarely saw automobiles on the quiet residential streets of N.D.G. but most youngsters knew the names of all the makes from collecting cigarette ads with pictures of all the latest models.

In the late 1920s and the early 1930s, when a group of boys was growing up on Old Orchard Avenue in the N.D.G. ward of Montreal, Great Britain was big. She ruled India, Burma and Ceylon, huge chunks of Africa, goodly pieces of South and Central America, and strategic locations around the world like Gibralter, Malta, Singapore, Hong Kong, and the Falkland Islands. Then there were the self-governing dominions like Canada, South Africa, Australia, and New Zealand. Britain ruled the seas. In return for this protection, she demanded and received major tariff concessions for her manufactured goods.

Because of the United States, British influence in Canada was probably much less than in other domains where sports such as cricket and rugger prevailed, and where people drove on the left-hand side of the road. In some categories, there was pretty good penetration in Canada. One of these was a popular fiction for boys and girls. *Chums Annual* was a hit at Christmas and weekly papers (we would call them comic books today) had good readership.

One of the Old Orchard boys received from his father a weekly subscription to two of these English comic books: *Triumph* and *Champion*. The whole group awaited the arrival of these papers each week. The stories were subdivided and devoured. There was 'King of Khyber Pass', where a master of disguise could be a rascally Pathan one minute and a

Tibetan monk the next. All this, of course, in the interest of doing the right thing: preserving and expanding the British sphere in India. There, Colwyn Dane and Slick Chester, a master detective and his assistant, would narrowly escape death each week. There were stories about public schools where no one could tell a lie and where cheating meant expulsion. There were daring exploits on the cliffs of Cornwall. Girls were never mentioned.

There was plenty to read with good old Tom Swift (*Call of the Wild*) and *White Fang* by Jack London, plus assorted westerns. There was always the hope at Christmas of getting *Chums* or *Boy's Own Annual.*

I do indeed remember G.A. Henty and some of his barn-burners like *With Buller in Natal* and *With Moore at Corunna.* What wonderful British propaganda we were all fed in those days, what with Henty and *Road to Mandalay* by Irving Cooper, and so many others.

Montreal's largest English newspapers were *The Gazette* in the morning, *The Herald*, which our fathers read at lunchtime, and *The Star*, which they brought home so our mothers could see the ads. We had *The Star*'s 'Burgess Bedtime' stories read to us when we were young but when we were older we read the sports page and the headlines about Lindberg's flight across the Atlantic in May 1927 and the visit of the R-100 airship in July 1930.

N.D.G. was home to a number of prominent sports figures. 'Howie' Morenz, flamboyant star of the Montreal Canadiens, lived on Girouard Avenue. 'Babe' Siebert of the Montreal Maroons bought his gas at Moxon's Service Station at the corner of Monkland and Oxford avenues, calling good-naturedly for service by banging the palm of his hand on the hood of his Windsor White Prince automobile. Aurel Joliat of the Canadiens operated a beer and grocery store in the ward for a time. 'Newsie' Lalonde, of an earlier hockey generation, could be seen on the Snowdon #83 streetcar. The Westward AAA on Royal Avenue sent up drop-kicking star 'Kenny' Copeland to the Winged Wheelers of the Big Four. Again on Royal Avenue, Hugh MacLennan, a great fan of the Canadiens, with a Ph.D. from Princeton University, later the author of the Canadian classic *Two Solitudes*, was teaching at Lower Canada College.

At the time, Montreal had two professional hockey teams: the Montreal Maroons and Les Canadiens. As English-speaking kids, we were more familiar with the names of 'Hooley' Smith, Nels Stewart and 'Babe' Siebert than with Howie Morenz or Aurel Joliat. We often argued over the merits of these teams. On Old Orchard, we formed a team called the 'Bulldogs'. We didn't win very often, but one victory is a vivid memory. Our team was a ragamuffin bunch in old odd sweaters. When our opponents in this game skated out, we gasped in awe -- they had uniforms! However, their sweaters didn't improve their skating and we won. Later, we managed to get team sweaters, too, but it did nothing to improve our play.

One hockey season around 1932, I remember sitting in the 'rush end' with 'Fritz' Pickering, Webster, 'Scotty' McDonald and 'Fat' Goodings to watch Morenz, et al. Fritz got upset at one of the referee's calls -- remember 'We want justice Marsh'? -- and pulled the rubber off one of his shoes and threw it out onto the ice. Very sheepishly, he had to obtain special permission to retrieve it after the game.

When we were all very young skaters, even those in the NHL wore flat blades as figure skaters do today. Then CCM came up with something new, 'Tube Skates'. Being much lighter, they were to add to a skater's speed. All that meant little to those of us stumbling around on weak ankles but it did bring about some awed comments of, "He got tube skates for Christmas!" when we gathered at the rink.

"TUBES"

When Doug Flutie made the first drop kick in 65 years in the National Football League, it was a reminder of the days when the emphasis was on the 'foot' in Canadian football, before the introduction of the forward pass with the MAAA's Warren Stevens. In those days punters were the big stars with the single point, the 'rouge' often decisive.

We tried drop kicking, which one could do alone, while place kicking needed a holder. The football trick Lucy would play on Charlie Brown didn't happen only in comic strips!

It was a hot afternoon late in August in the 1930s. The kid from Old Orchard Avenue was bored. Everybody was away. There was nothing to do. Finally he hopped on his bike and pedalled over to the YMCA on Royal Avenue. He kicked his toe in the outfield dust. There was nothing to do here, either.

Then the door of the clubhouse swung open. An older boy came out. He was tall. Square jawed. Scandinavian looking. He said "Yup" like Gary Cooper. His name was Herbie Westman. He carried a football.

Herbie Westman was the star kicker for the West Hill High School football team, taking them to a city title. He was a local hero. Later, he led the McGill Redmen to an Intercollegiate championship. Summer evenings he pitched for the Westmount Owls down at Atwater Park. He looked around when he came out of the clubhouse and seeing nobody else there, said to the kid from Old Orchard Avenue, "Wanna kick this back and forth?" Silly question.

The kid caught Herbie Westman's towering punts and returned them. To this day he remembers that he had never, before or since, kicked a football so far. Finally, Herbie Westman said quietly, "Gotta go home for supper." He left and the session was over.

Over the years the kid from Old Orchard Avenue saw Howie Morenz play hockey at the Forum. He saw Maurice Richard receive a six-minute ovation at the Molson Centre. He saw Sam Snead play golf at the Royal Montreal Golf Club. But it was never like kicking a football with Herbie Westman....

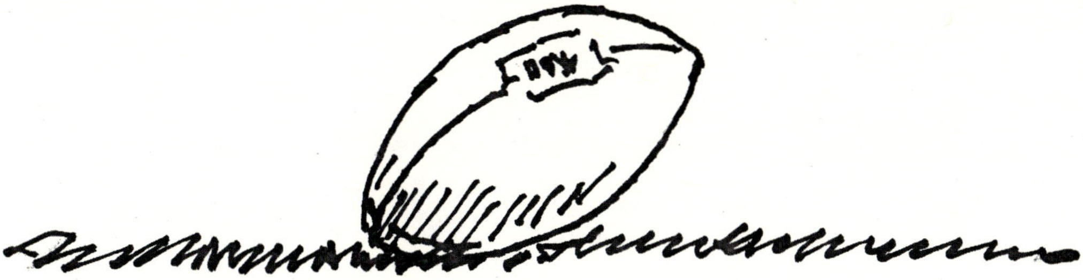

The Westward Amateur Athletic Association owned property on Royal Avenue in N.D.G. The property consisted of a football field with a small wooden grandstand, tennis courts and a clubhouse. During the 1930s, there were lots of young men frustrated by the lack of jobs or poor wages who found an outlet in football. Westward found the players easily; what was hard to find was money for sweaters and helmets. For funding, the executive decided to hold a fair.

Booths were set up to provide refreshments and games of chance. A public address system was installed, and, much to the dismay of nearby residents, the hit song of the day, 'Around the Corner and Under the Tree, the Sergeant Major Made Love to Me', was played loud and clear and often. Teenagers loved the fair.

One evening, this writer and his friend George Pope were walking around the booths when they noticed that one of the prizes at the Wheel of Fortune was a pair of pigeons. This gave rise to visions of raising and racing these birds. The Bains' back porch seemed suitable for this purpose. The dream was allowed to ferment for a day or two. Then, we returned to the fair with enough money for one ticket, certain that this would be our lucky day. We debated and decided on the number, and then the choice was made. The wheel stopped far from our selection.

The disappointment was heavy, but on the way home, we talked about buying a breeding pair of rabbits at the Bonsecours Market to be housed in the Popes' basement. The senior Popes stamped on this plan and we bought ourselves a half-dozen horse chestnuts, each of which we strung on a shoelace to play 'breakers'.

On the northeast corner of Girouard and Notre Dame de Grâce Avenues, there was a big open tract of land. Back from the street on this site, there was a hut that was home to a lone, eccentric old man with long white hair. 'The Hermit' could be seen out for walks of a summer's evening in a pair of shorts and Alpine boots, with a parrot on his shoulder. Conspicuous, to say the least, in the middle class suburb, The Hermit was said to be an English remittance man. Out of step though he may have been, the old man kept a marvellous garden full of flowers and vegetables that were prized in the district.

After supper, many a father would either take his kids over in the family touring car, or walk with them, towing Junior's wagon, up the short dirt road to the eccentric's hut where they would fill a basket or two with fresh tomatoes, beans, Golden Bantam corn, onions, and some fresh-cut flowers. In autumn, The Hermit would sell horse chestnuts to schoolboys, who would then string one chestnut on a knotted shoelace and play a game at recess known as 'breakers'. Later, the old man, who was only squatting on the land, had to yield his way of life to the community's need, and the Daniel O'Connell School was constructed on the property.

With snow removal being done by manpower -- that is, man and horse power -- streets were left with a covering of snow for sleighs to travel on. Sidewalks were cleared by a one-man horse plow. This left large piles of snow in front of houses -- ideal for youngsters' winter fun. We made snowmen and snowballs and built snow forts. We raided each other's forts with much throwing of snowballs and yelling of challenges. The day would end with a snow-covered bunch of kids heading for home for energy-restoring hot Bovril.

SNOW FORTS
AND SNOWBALLS

REMEMBER
SNOW REMOVAL
BEFORE
MECHANIZATION
OR SALT?

These were the days of the home delivery -- everything came right to the doorstep. The vegetable man toured our streets in summer and the grocery cart came to the door, too. There was the milkman early in the morning, the bread man, too. The most important to the youngsters was the ice man. On hot summer days we followed the ice wagon. While the man was delivering the blocks of ice to people's ice boxes, we would scramble into the back of the wagon to claim slivers of ice left over from his chipping with an ice pick. Sucking these bits of ice was our refreshing treat of a lazy summer afternoon.

DO YOU REMEMBER MILK BOTTLES DELIVERED TO YOUR DOOR ?
OR THE FROZEN CREAM AT THE TOP ?
LOVED BY LITTLE KIDS AND CATS

REMEMBER THE OLD BREAD WAGON
WITH ITS LOAD OF "GOODIES"
PIES CAKES AND BUNS

The GROCERY DELIVERY SLEIGH

Remember
the BREAD WAGON?
Home delivery
of Bread,
rolls, cake
and the slam
of the doors
as he loaded
his basket
and the horse
that knew the
route

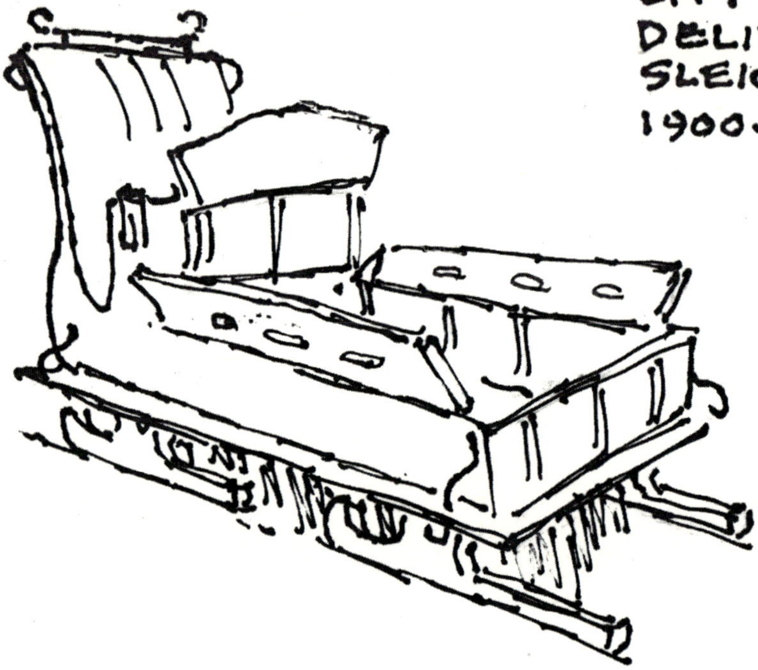

CITY
DELIVERY
SLEIGH
1900–1920

Remember Sleigh-Bells?
Some were on the harness and some on the shafts —
I recall hearing them as we played street hockey on dull winter afternoons.

Most men in N.D.G. drank Molson's Export Ale. Remember newscaster Christopher Ellis and his 'long green bottles'? There were cartoon newspaper ads asking, 'Where's Joe?' It seems he had gone for a Dow Ale. There was Dawes Black Horse Ale at the grocery store. Women sipped Salada or Orange pekoe tea. On festive occasions there was Montreal's own Gurd's Ginger Ale.

In the 1930s, Ida Steinberg opened a grocery store on Monkland Avenue near Harvard. David Dunsmore, who now lives in Agincourt, Ontario, worked for her as a delivery boy in those years. He remembers how Ida loved to show the shopping housewives which vegetables were prime, and how, even when Sam Steinberg visited the store, everyone knew that red-haired Ida was the boss. Dunsmore worked long hours for his $2.50 per day, always under the threat from Ida that his pay would be docked if he dawdled on his deliveries. But to this day, he swears by that fiery lady's business sense and integrity.

The CORNER GROCERY STORE AND THE DELIVERY BOY'S BIKE

For most kids of the '20s and '30s a trip to the corner candy store was a big treat. Standing in front of the penny-candy case debating whether to pick something that could be swallowed quickly or a more lasting one to suck on was a big problem. There was so much to choose from -- shiny black licorice whips and pipes, honeymoons, milk bottles, jelly beans, and jawbreakers of all sizes. All this and the delay while the shopkeeper waited patiently. But the ultimate treat was a trip to Elmhurst Dairy for an ice cream cone. All N.D.G. was firmly convinced that Elmhurst was the world's best and on a summer day who would argue?

Do you remember a candy store that we frequented on Monkland near Old Orchard? I can remember Bill Whelan going into the shop with a nickel and driving the old woman -- Mrs. Cameron, I think -- nearly crazy. With honeymoons at two for a cent, he would buy one, then with caramels at four for a cent he would buy two and so it went through jelly beans and licorice sticks.

Long before LPs, CDs or teenagers with earphones plugged into the latest pop tunes, many families had a Victrola in the home -- remember His Master's Voice? Outside all we heard were the clip-clop of horses' hooves or the toot of auto horns. There were organ grinders downtown but they didn't venture as far as N.D.G. One had his post at the corner in front of Morgan's department store, grinding out his old familiar tunes in hopes of reward from passing shoppers.

When we were very young the biggest treat was being taken downtown to see Santa Claus at Eaton's or Morgan's department stores. If we had been especially good we rated a trip to watch the big Eaton's Santa Claus parade.

May first was the traditional Montreal moving day when people moved from one flat to another. In N.D.G. you would see the big trucks of Baillargeon and Meldrum the Mover. We were lucky on Old Orchard Avenue that we stayed together so long. The beauty of a street gang was that everybody got on a team even if in hockey you spent a lot of time standing in the snow by the boards freezing your feet.

One of the big days of the year was the 24th of May, Queen Victoria's birthday. We sang;

The 24th of May
The Queen's birthday
If you don't give us a holiday
We'll all run away.

Then we spent the day lighting firecrackers of various sizes and intensity, creating the kind of din little boys enjoy. At night fathers fired the skyrockets and Roman Candles to the Oohs and Aahs of delighted youngsters watching the glittering night sky.

CARTIERVILLE
CAR APPROACHING
SNOWDON JUNCTION

DO YOU
REMEMBER
SNOWDON
JUNCTION?
THE TRAM CIRCLE
WHERE CARS SET OFF
FOR OUTREMONT, DOWN
TOWN MONTREAL
and
IN SUMMER
THE
CARTIERVILLE
CAR
OVER THE
FIELDS TO
BELMONT
PARK!
FROM A SKETCH OF 1940

The streetcar was very important to Montrealers in the first half of the 20th century. They rode it to work in the morning and came home at night, frequently hanging on the back doors of open-end trams at rush hour. There were two-man crews, one man crews and even the 'Golden Chariot' to take tourists around the mountain. For kids on Old Orchard Avenue the big thrill was when the workers laid the tracks on Monkland Avenue. It was more fun than a circus to watch the men and equipment laying rails and paving the street with us having ringside seats for it all.

The "GOLDEN CHARIOT"

SNOWDON JUNCTION

Streetcars were our link to everywhere in the west end. We had the #3 running west along Sherbrooke Street past the fields of Benny Farm all the way to Montreal West. Tickets were four for a quarter for adults and school tickets seven for a quarter -- you needed a school pass for these. The #83 went along Girouard Avenue to Snowdon Junction where you could transfer to the Cartierville car for the ride over the fields to Belmont Park for a day of fun with cotton candy, hotdogs and roller coaster rides.

The girls of N.D.G. were quite neatly clothed. In winter many wore Red River coats while the boys' costumes were more eclectic -- shirts and ties but sweaters of wild and wonderful colour combinations. Some teachers inspected the shine on our shoes, which often proved inadequate so stay-after-school orders would be given. In winter we incurred official displeasure by wearing moccasins or ski boots. When we arrived in high school, dress was more formal -- jackets and flannels for boys and uniforms for girls. We all heaved a sigh of relief when term ended and more casual clothes were the style. This was long before anyone dreamed of T-shirts or blue jeans as a universal costume.

One of the big moments in a boy's life was the graduation from 'breeks' to long pants. Breeks were the style of breeches usually made of corduroy, which after being wet, dried stiff as a board. Long pants didn't make a man of you but it meant you were on your way.

Every fall we headed to the store with that school supplies list for exercise books, pencils, rulers, and the awful '292' pen nib. We usually bought textbooks from somebody a grade ahead. Books with hand-drawn illustrations by a previous owner were in great demand.

Our days at West Hill High School coincided with the term of Charles Rittenhouse as a teacher of English literature and drama. One of our group, Bill Whelan, received a role in a Rittenhouse production of 'Romeo and Juliet'. He played Friar Lawrence while another friend, Ivor Francis, played Romeo. Ivor went on to perform professionally in the United States while Bill was left with his dreams of acting glory.

Those days we read ***The Monitor***, a weekly paper delivered free to our doorsteps. The paper featured stories about two young N.D.G. boys, Johnny Coy and Tom Auburn. Coy was a dancer who we never heard of again while Tom Auburn became 'Magic Tom', who entertained and mystified generations of Montrealers.

The other night as we channel-surfed the TV we came across a re-run of 'Lou Grant'. At one point Mavis shouted, "There's Ivor Francis!" Sure enough, there he was, cast as a rejected husband in a bar scene. Our old friend....

A welcome addition to our school life was the 'chip wagon'. Long before Mayor Drapeau banned them from our streets they used to come around at recess and lunch time. No school football game was complete without a chip wagon parked nearby.

For quite a few years they have been silent. For all of our youthful days we heard the bells of St. Augustine's church ringing in the skies of Notre Dame de Grâce. Their peals were part of N.D.G. life, especially for the many Masses on Sundays. Then the large impressive building just to the north of N.D.G. Park stood empty, its congregation scattered. Also scattered were the furnishings, including the bells, which had been donated by the Kindellan family. The building is now occupied by the River's Edge Community Church.

Many youngsters who grew up in N.D.G. have left to seek their fortunes elsewhere. Many have stayed in Montreal. A new generation of youngsters is now growing up here. They may have electronic toys instead of 'breakers' but the streets, homes and churches are the same. Members of Russ Bain's and John Collins' generation remember the spirit of the neighbourhood of their youth. But whatever the age, they all are members of that greater community who can proudly say, "I'm from N.D.G. !!"

About the Author

Russell Bain and John Collins grew up together in N.D.G, attending Herbert Simon Elementary and West Hill High School.

From boyhood, Russell showed an interest in writing and in his teens worked for the *N.D.G. Monitor*.

He joined the Army in World War II and served overseas for five years in England and the Continent. He was 'Mentioned in Dispatches' and discharged as a captain at the end of the war.

He married Mavis Barwick, also of N.D.G., in 1946 and they had a daughter and a son. They lived in Montreal for 25 years, where he worked in menswear and became president of the B.V.D. Shirt Company.

In 1972, he and Mavis moved to Kingston. Besides his writing, Russell enjoyed golf, curling and cottage life until his death in 2004.

About the Artist

After high school, John attended l'Ecole des Beaux Arts and Sir George Williams College. He married Edna Fischer, of Montreal West.

For over 40 years he was editorial cartoonist of the *Montreal Gazette* and illustrated Edgar Andrew Collard's column, "All Our Yesterdays". He also illustrated five of Mr. Collard's books.

John was a member of the Lakeshore Association of Artists. His paintings are in public and private collections here and abroad. He is represented in Montreal by the Westend Gallery in Westmount. He lived with Edna in Dorval until his death in September 2007.

John Collins' first book was *Montreal Memories of the Century from the Sketchbooks of John Collins, 2000.* His second, in 2004, was *Quebec Sketchbook, 1940-2004: Over 60 Years of Sketching our City and our Province: From the Sketchbooks of John Collins.* They and *Growing up in N.D.G.* have been published by Shoreline.